Art Works™ Drawing Things That Go

Carolyn Scrace

A⁺
Smart Apple Media

Author:
Carolyn Scrace graduated from Brighton College of Art, England, after studying design and illustration. She has since worked in animation, advertising, and children's publishing. She has a special interest in natural history and has written many books on the subject, including *Lion Journal* and *Gorilla Journal* in the *Animal Journal* series.

How to use this book:

Follow the easy, numbered instructions. Simple step-by-step stages enable budding young artists to create their own amazing drawings.

What you will need:

1. Paper.
2. Wax crayons.
3. Felt-tip pens to add color.

Published by Smart Apple Media, an imprint of Black Rabbit Books
P.O. Box 3263, Mankato, Minnesota 56002
www.blackrabbitbooks.com

Published by arrangement with
The Salariya Book Company Ltd

Cataloging-in-Publication Data is available from the Library of Congress

Printed in the United States
At Corporate Graphics,
North Mankato, Minnesota

9 8 7 6 5 4 3 2

ISBN: 978-1-62588-348-3

Contents

Rocket

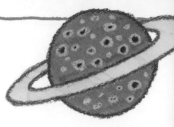

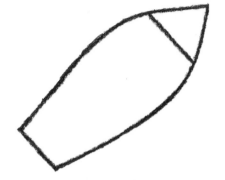

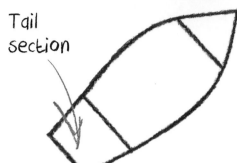

Tail section

1 A rocket needs a nose cone,

2 ...a body,

3 ...a tail section,

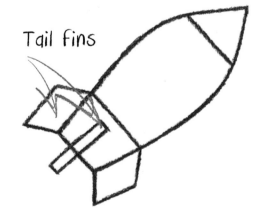

Tail fins

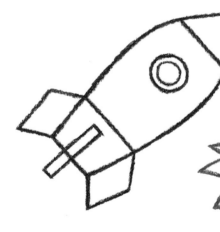

4 ...three tail fins,

5 ...and a window.

6 Now draw in some flames!

4

Draw some stars.

Draw a planet with craters.

Color in with felt-tip pens.

5

Boat

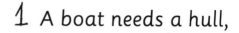

1 A boat needs a hull,

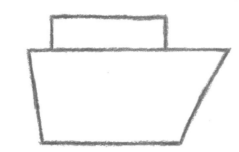

2 ...a cabin,

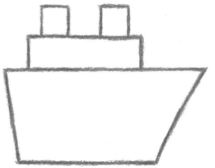

3 ...two funnels,

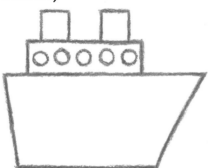

4 ...and five portholes.

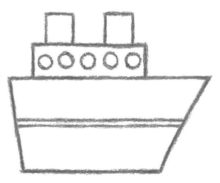

5 Draw in two stripes on the hull.

6 Then add **lots** of waves!

Draw smoke coming out of both funnels.

Add a stripe to each funnel.

Draw in an anchor.

Anchor

Color in with felt-tip pens.

7

Airplane

1 An airplane needs a body,

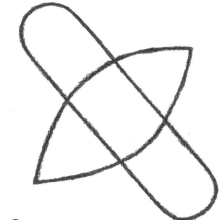

2 ...two wings,

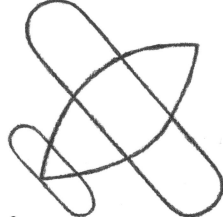

3 ...a tail,

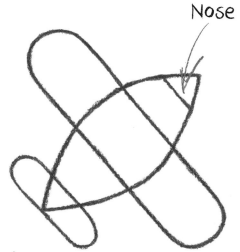

Nose

4 ...a nose section,

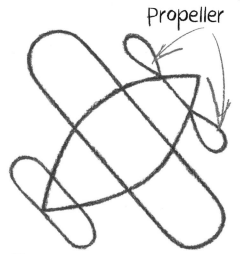

Propeller

5 ...and a propeller.

Cockpit

6 Draw in the cockpit.

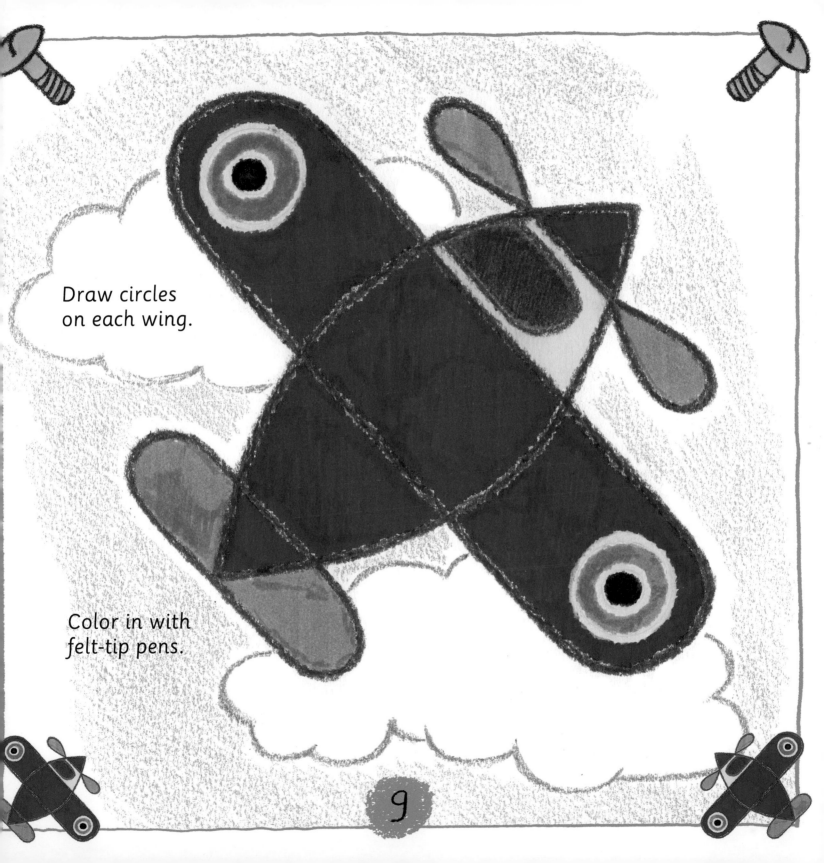

Draw circles on each wing.

Color in with felt-tip pens.

9

Car

1 A car needs a body,

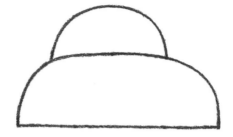

2 ...a roof,

3 ...two wheels,

4 ...and a door and handle.

5 Draw in windows,

Bumper   Bumper

6 ...and two bumpers!

10

Now draw in the
steering wheel.

Steering
wheel

Color in with
felt-tip pens.

11

Digger

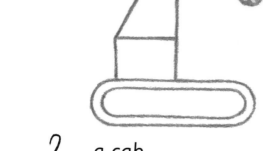

Caterpillar tracks

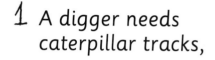

1 A digger needs caterpillar tracks,

2 ...a cab,

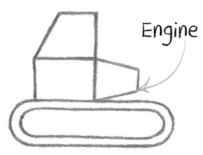

Engine

3 ...an engine,

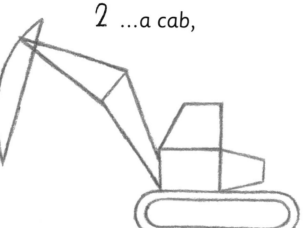

4 ...and a **long** arm.

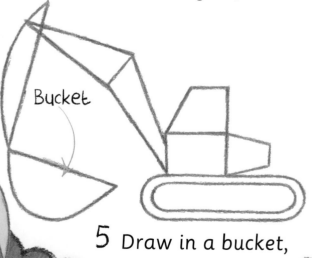

Bucket

5 Draw in a bucket,

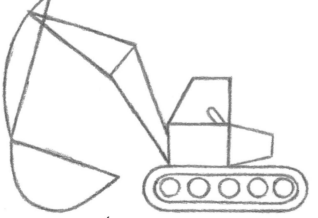

6 ...and some wheels.

12

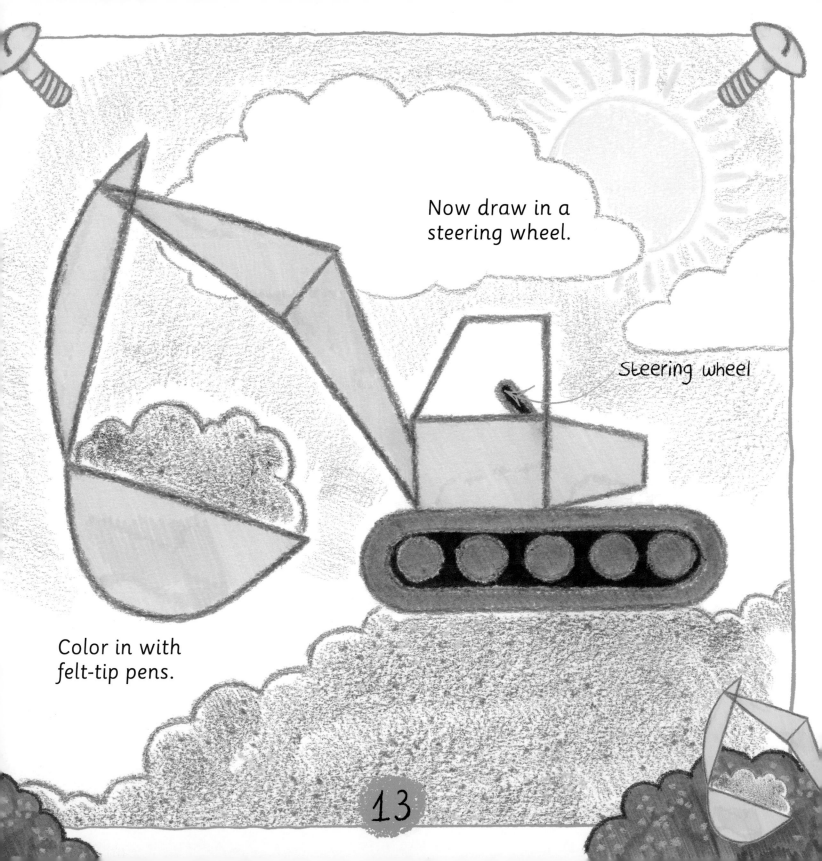

Tractor

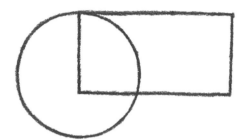

1 A tractor needs a body,

2 ...a very **big** back wheel,

3 ...a small front wheel,

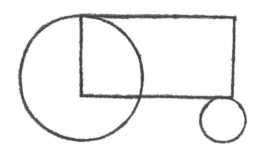

Exhaust pipe

4 ...and a driver's cab.

5 Now draw in a steering wheel,

6 ...and an exhaust pipe!

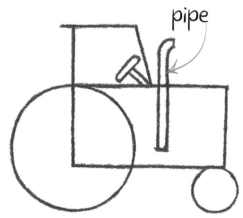

Add tires to the tractor wheels.

Hubcaps

Draw in hubcaps to finish off the wheels.

Color in with felt-tip pens.

15

 # Helicopter

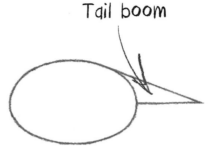

Tail boom

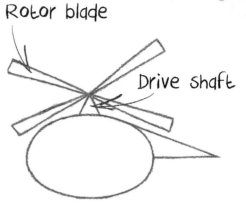

Rotor blade

Drive shaft

1 A helicopter needs a body,

2 ...a tail boom,

3 ...a drive shaft with **four** rotor blades,

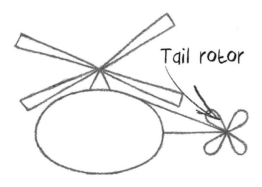

Tail rotor

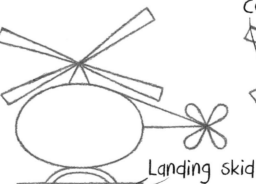

Landing skid

Cockpit

4 ...and a tail rotor!

5 Now draw in the landing skid,

6 ...and the cockpit.

16

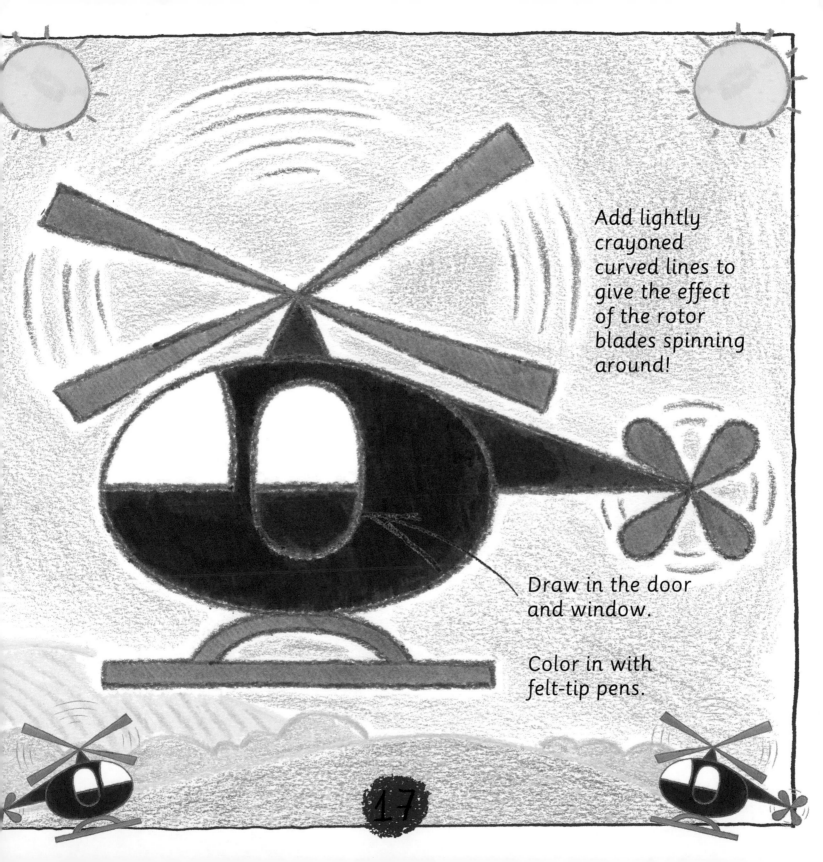

Add lightly
crayoned
curved lines to
give the effect
of the rotor
blades spinning
around!

Draw in the door
and window.

Color in with
felt-tip pens.

Truck

Trailer

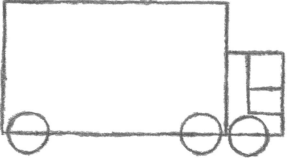

1 A truck needs a cab,

2 ...a **big** trailer,

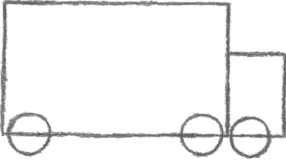

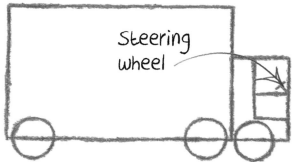

3 ...and three wheels.

4 Draw in the cab door and window,

Steering wheel

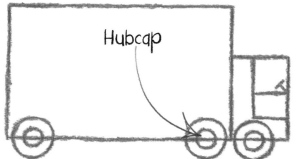

Hubcap

5 ...and add a steering wheel.

6 Draw in the hubcaps.

Draw in a door handle.

Door handle

Color in with felt-tip pens.

19

Fire Truck

1 A fire truck needs a cab,

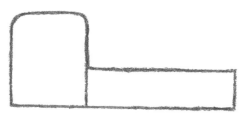

2 ...a long rear section,

3 ...and three wheels.

Cradle

Arm

4 Draw in the cab door and windows.

Lifting device

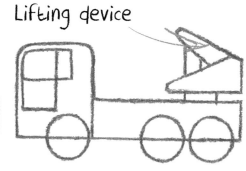

5 Add a lifting device at the back,

6 ...with a **long** arm and cradle.

Finish off the arm
with a crayoned
zigzag line.

Draw in the
light and the
steering wheel.

Draw in the
reel and hose.

Add hubcaps.

Color in with
felt-tip pens.

21

Train

Boiler

1 A train needs a body,

2 ...a boiler,

3 ...three wheels,

4 ...and a roof, door, and window.

Draw in some carriages and add **lots** of windows.

Tender

5 A train needs a tender,

6 ...and the tender needs a roof and wheels.

7 Draw in a rounded front end.

Finish off the wheel section.

Wheel section

Color in with felt-tip pens.

Bus

1 A bus needs a body,

2 ...a roof,

3 ...a side panel,

4 ...and doors.

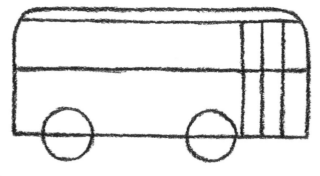

5 Now draw in two wheels,

6 ...and **lots** of windows!

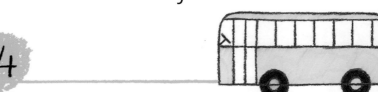

Draw in a steering wheel.

Add the hubcaps.

Color in with felt-tip pens.

25

 # Snowplow

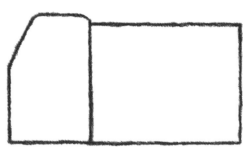

1 A snowplow needs a cab,

2 ...a body,

3 ...and three wheels.

Plow blade

4 Draw in the plow blade.

5 Add a door and windows,

Salt carrier

6 ...and a line for the salt carrier.

Draw in a
flashing light!

Add a steering wheel.

Crayon in
hubcaps.

Color in with
felt-tip pens.

27

 # Bicycle

Handlebars

Front fork

1 A bicycle needs a frame,

2 ...two wheels,

3 ...a front fork with handlebars,

Back fork   Saddle

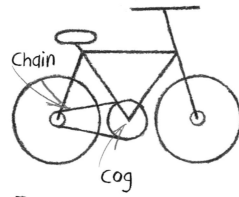
Chain

Cog

Pedals

4 ...a back fork, and a saddle.

5 Draw in a round cog, and a chain,

6 ...and two pedals.

Tire

Draw in the tires
and lots of spokes.

Spoke

Color in with
felt-tip pens.

 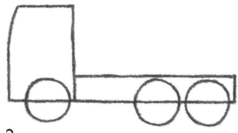

Cement Mixer

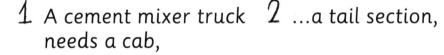

1 A cement mixer truck needs a cab,

2 ...a tail section,

3 ...and three wheels.

Exhaust pipe

Mixing drum

Rear pedestal

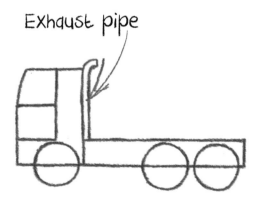  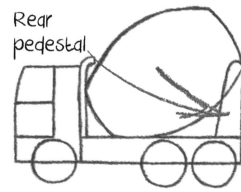

4 Draw in the cab door and window. Add an exhaust pipe!

5 Now draw in a **big** mixing drum,

6 ...and a rear pedestal.

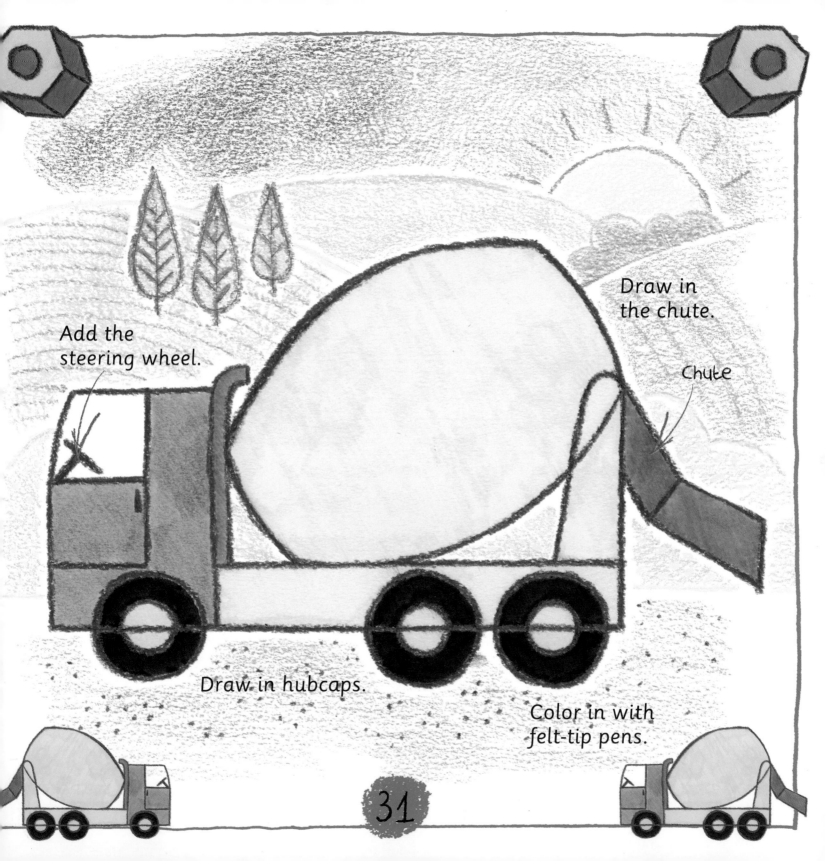

Draw in
the chute.

Chute

Add the
steering wheel.

Draw in hubcaps.

Color in with
felt-tip pens.

31

Glossary

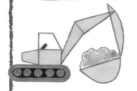

Boiler the part of a steam engine where water is boiled to make steam.

Caterpillar track a track made of metal or rubber plates joined together. Vehicles with these tracks can go over rough ground easily.

Cockpit the part of an airplane where the pilot sits.

Exhaust pipe the part of a vehicle where the exhaust smoke comes out.

Rotor blades the big propeller on the top of a helicopter which makes it go up and down.

Tail fins the short wings at the back of a rocket or airplane.

Tender a truck carrying coal and water that goes behind a steam engine.

Index